THE JIGSAW BOOK

Hutchinson & Co. (Publishers) Ltd
An imprint of the Hutchinson Publishing Group
3 Fitzroy Square, London W1P 6JD

Hutchinson Group (Australia) Pty Ltd
30–32 Cremorne Street, Richmond South, Victoria 3121
PO Box 151, Broadway, New South Wales 2007

Hutchinson Group (NZ) Ltd
32–34 View Road, PO Box 40-086, Glenfield, Auckland 10

Hutchinson Group (SA) (Pty) Ltd
PO Box 337, Bergvlei 2012, South Africa

First published in 1981

Text of book © Linda Hannas 1981

This volume © Bellew & Higton Publishers Ltd 1981

Designed and produced for Hutchinson & Co. by
Bellew & Higton Publishers Ltd
19–21 Conway Street, London W1P 6JD

Printed and bound in Scotland by Morrison & Gibb Ltd
Typeset in 12pt. Horley Old Style by
MFK Graphic Systems (Typesetting) Ltd, Saffron Walden, Essex
ISBN 0 09 145541 3

Linda Hannas
THE JIGSAW BOOK

Hutchinson of London

CONTENTS

Dorothy Comingore doing a Parker Brothers puzzle
in the film of *Citizen Kane* 1941.

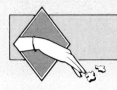

THE HISTORY OF JIGSAW PUZZLES

Walk into a room where a half-completed jigsaw puzzle lies spread out on a table and you will probably be strongly tempted to try to fit in a piece or two. Why? What is it about the jigsaw puzzle that exerts so irresistible a force on old and young alike?

Puzzles have been designed to instil moral values in young children and to titillate jaded adults; they have been cut into huge straight-sided pieces for the very young and into thousands of tiny interlocking bits for more sophisticated puzzle addicts. Made from mahogany, cardboard, plastic, softwood, plywood, even

gingerbread and solid silver, they have been used for education, amusement, propaganda and escapism. Their appeal is universal and timeless, and yet they have only been in existence for two centuries.

Jigsaw puzzles were invented in about 1760 to lighten the severities of eighteenth-century education. John Locke, the philosopher, had written that he had 'always had a fancy that learning might be a play and recreation to children', and by the second half of the century his ideas were taking root in the minds of book publishers and educationalists. It was, however, the

brainchild of a young map-maker that eventually brought play into the schoolroom.

He was John Spilsbury, owner of a print shop at Russell Court in Covent Garden. In those days any print shop was a fascinating place, but Spilsbury's was livelier than most. Imagine it: there would have been maps and charts, all manner of stationery, almanacs, bibles cheek by jowl with new plays, prints to suit every taste and pocket, and boxes and boxes of 'dissected maps'. He used to mount beautifully engraved, hand-coloured and embellished maps on sheets of mahogany and, with a fine marquetry saw, dissect them along the boundaries of countries and counties, in effect making the first jigsaw puzzles.

There were no children's toyshops in eighteenth-century London, and, apart from Spilsbury's dissected maps, the only products specifically made for children were tiny, illustrated books, bound in pretty floral covers. Customers flocked to Russell Court to see the new invention. John shared the premises with his brother Jonathan, a fashionable portrait painter (his most famous subject was probably George III) whose aristocratic clients would drop into the print shop to buy the latest novelties.

This was the great era of the Grand Tour, when a man's social status could be measured by his knowledge of geography. The poet William Cowper went as far as to say: 'Geography is a science essentially necessary to the accomplishment of a gentleman, yet it is imperfectly, if at all, inculcated in schools.' It was for this reason that Spilsbury dissected his maps. In his second trade card he advertised: 'All sorts of Dissected Maps for Teaching Geography', and in 1763 a London Street Directory listed him as: 'Engraver and Map Dissector in Wood, in order to facilitate the Teaching of Geography.' The puzzles were

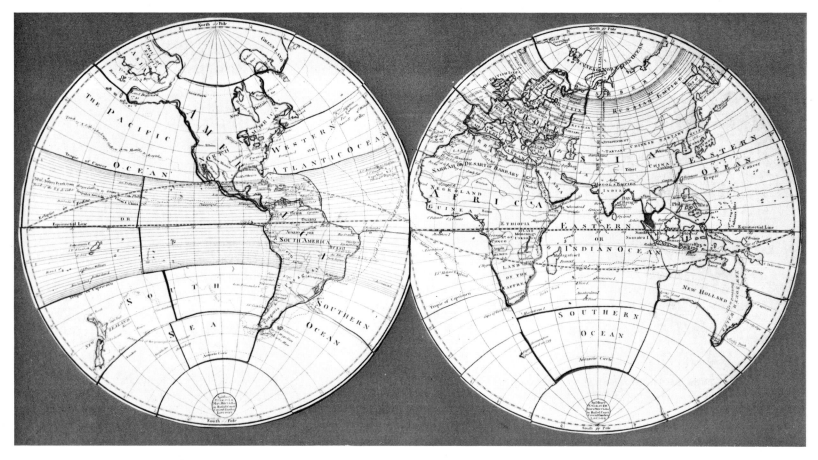

The World. John Spilsbury *c.*1760. One of the first dissected maps made by the inventor of the jigsaw puzzle.

undoubtedly successful. In 1786 Cowper was writing to a friend: 'When Lord Spencer's son was four years old [that is, in 1762] he knew the situation of every Kingdom, country, county, city and river in the world. For this attainment he was indebted to a plaything, having been accustomed to amuse himself with those maps which are cut into several compartments, so as to be thrown into a heap of confusion, that they may be put together again with an exact coincidence of all their angles and bearings, so as to form a perfect whole.'

Such a tortuous description suggests that Cowper thought his friend had never heard of dissected maps, although by then they had been on sale for a quarter of a century. Of course, they were very expensive; Spilsbury's later trade card devoted to puzzles lists two prices: 10s 6d for a superior puzzle 'square in a square box' or 7s 6d 'without the sea in a chip box'. The sea was not considered very important and was generally cut at random into large pieces, but it required a lot of very expensive wood. The

extravagant rectangular puzzles were sold in well-made oak boxes, while the others, irregularly shaped without the sea, were packaged in the thin oval boxes used for all kinds of knick-knacks at that time. It is not very surprising that the puzzles cost so much (more than an agricultural worker's weekly wage), because they were entirely hand-made from expensive materials.

Jane Austen, always ready to make fun of snobbery and pretension, caricatured self-righteous puzzle-owners in *Mansfield Park*: 'As her cousins found her ignorant of many things with which they had long since been familiar, they thought her prodigiously stupid ... and were continually bringing some fresh report of it into the drawing room. "Dear Mama, only think, my cousin cannot put the map of Europe together."'

When Spilsbury died, just before his thirtieth birthday, his assistant Harry Ashby took over the business. He continued to make and sell dissected maps for a while, but without Spilsbury he soon lost interest and closed the shop. Other cartographers were not so dismissive, and several of them cashed in on Spilsbury's invention, adding a useful refinement. The earliest puzzles had had no interlocking pieces, which meant that the

Before and After Marriage. John Wallis 1789. Turn the book upside down to see why this is unusually frivolous for so early a puzzle.

slightest jerk or slip would scatter the assembled map. Spilsbury's imitators continued to dissect the maps precisely along the boundaries, but they cut the borders into interlocking pieces to give the puzzles some stability. It was more than twenty years, however, before it occurred to anyone to dissect anything other than maps. Even in 1775 when a large London print shop catalogued hundreds of prints, it was only of the maps that they wrote: 'Any may be had dissected, on Boards.'

When new subjects did emerge, they were still intended for education. There were puzzles with forbidding rows of kings and queens, or Old Testament prophets, each tiny picture heading lists of useful facts and dates. The pieces still did not interlock and, as the pictures did not overlap the cutting lines, they were extremely difficult to put together unless the assembler knew the correct order of the kings or prophets.

In 1785 a really light-hearted puzzle was published at last, and it explains why William Cowper was so knowledgeable about dissections in the following year. It was an illustration of his ballad 'John Gilpin' and was published by John Wallis. As a map-maker, Wallis had started his career dissecting maps like all the others, but he was far too imaginative to restrict himself to such sober subjects. His chief rival over the next fifty years was William Darton. Their shops were almost next door to each other, their material equally good, but their approach was amusingly different. Darton, in 1787, was the first to dissect a chronological table of English Kings, and a very slow, stodgy puzzle it was. But Wallis, after his success with *Johnny Gilpin of*

Cheapside, borrowed Darton's idea, transforming it into something much simpler and more colourful. Not surprisingly Wallis's version was much more popular, and he was still producing copies of it ten years later.

In 1790 Wallis turned to race games. These had been invented by the Italians in the sixteenth century and though their popularity had fluctuated, it had never lapsed completely. At the time of John Spilsbury's apprenticeship an enterprising map-maker had designed a geographical race game, but it had not sold. Such games did not become popular until the 1770s, when other manufacturers poured more and more into the shops to satisfy the growing demand. In spite of his map-making training, Wallis again broke from the geographical straitjacket. This time he turned to France and called his version of a traditional French game *The New Game of Human Life*. With its eighty-four finely engraved and delicately coloured scenes in the life of man from babyhood to the grave, it was very popular. Encouraged by his success, Wallis dissected it and sold it as a puzzle, the first in a long tradition of puzzle-games.

The dissectors' rivalry had grown to such proportions by 1812 that Wallis engraved labels for his puzzles declaring that 'John Wallis the original Manufacturer of Dissected Maps and Puzzles (having dedicated full 30 years to that particular line of business) requests the Public to Observe that all his dissected articles are superior both in correctness and workmanship to any in London, and none are genuine but what are signed on the label, John Wallis'. It is just possible that Wallis had never seen or heard of Spilsbury's dissected maps, for Spilsbury had died in 1769 and

Two pieces from *Teaching the Elements of History and Chronology.* C. Dilly and William Darton 1787.

The print shop at Sidmouth to which young John Wallis was banished by his father.

Wallis did not produce any puzzles until 1785 (his claim of 'full 30 years' was a little exaggerated), but it is more likely that he staked his claim on the assumption that everybody else would have forgotten poor Spilsbury. If so, his assumption was correct and even twentieth-century toy historians have accepted his claim and have referred to him as the inventor of the jigsaw puzzle.

He had two sons, the younger of whom, Edward, worked with his father; the elder was apparently distrusted and banished to Sidmouth. William Darton had sons too, Samuel and William, but none of Wallis's paranoia. Samuel joined his father's business in Gracechurch Street at the end of the eighteenth century, while his brother set up independently on nearby Holborn Hill in 1804. Both businesses flourished and remained in the Darton family until the 1860s. They were Quakers and their beliefs were reflected in their wares. The elder William published many dissected puzzles of the soberer sort, but not a single race game, which would have smacked too much of chance and gambling.

He also brought out many children's books, some of which he wrote and illustrated himself. *Twinkle, Twinkle Little Star* by Jane and Anne Taylor was first issued by him, as was a poem called 'My Mother'. This so took the public's fancy that his son made a puzzle of it, each verse prettily illustrated. The ever-watchful Wallis saw its success and produced a very similar one called *My Sister*, which sold just as well to a public credulous enough to think it was by the same author.

The younger William's Holborn firm produced a huge range of juvenile material, including books on the 'Arts, Sciences and Polite Literature' as well as innumerable educational puzzles, priced between 2s 6d and 10s. Shrinking from the strident claims of his non-Quaker competitor, he printed a warning that he could not 'recommend as Instructive any Dissections which sell at less than 2s 6d'. But he was not above a little advertising in his children's books. In one story a character says: 'I know Mr. DARTON of London has published some [dissected maps] upon a new plan, in which every care has been taken to make them perfectly correct.' It is true that the Darton puzzles were very carefully made from scrupulously chosen subjects.

A brother-Quaker, Daniel Wheeler, believed that God wished him to leave the comfort of his English farm, but had no idea where the call would lead him until one day his eye fell on the pieces of his children's dissected map. Seeing St Petersburg lying apart from the rest he suddenly had the feeling that God was calling him to Russia. He braved the rigours of a long Russian winter awaiting a summons; in due course Tsar Alexander requested his help with a drainage scheme for St Petersburg and he successfully drained 3,000 acres of marsh and swamp. Outside Leningrad there is still a monument to him, though not to the puzzle which sent him there.

In England the second half of the nineteenth century saw the final emergence of puzzles for pleasure untainted with didacticism. The cutting remained simple and the engravings were generally hand-coloured, but at last puzzles were being produced solely for amusement. Scripture and history puzzles were still available, but even they were reminiscent of Boswell's attempt to be a philosopher: 'cheerfulness was always breaking through.' They were still only intended for children, but some adults enjoyed them. In her journal Queen Victoria described an evening spent assembling dissected pictures with Lord Melbourne and Lord Conyngham as 'the pleasantest gayest evening I have passed for some time. I sat up until $\frac{1}{2}$ past 11.' The range of subjects and quality was enormous; the good, the bad and the indifferent were made by established firms, fly-by-night manufacturers out for a quick profit and amateurs. There was even a tailor in the City of London who used to dissect puzzles in his back room when times were bad and no one wanted new clothes.

Right: postage-stamp portrait of J. W. Barfoot and far right: one of his puzzles, *The Star of the West c.* 1865. The heroine of this unusual puzzle is probably either the American actress Adah Isaacs Menken or 'Skittles' (the courtesan Catherine Walters).

In this atmosphere the last of the great family firms of puzzle-makers grew and prospered. It is a firm that can only be described as bizarre, because of its astonishing obsession with anonymity. Its puzzles were sold through retailers whose lists carried no identifying name or address. The puzzles were never signed or advertised, and yet they dominated the Victorian scene. Some of them were tiny, with no more than twenty pieces, selling from 1s 6d; others (costing 10s) were huge, made from wood a thumbnail thick, with a map on one side and an amusing picture on the other. The cutting ignored the map boundaries and concentrated on the pretty picture.

In fact the firm consisted of another father and son, who were not unmasked until the early 1970s, when the author of this book tracked them down to 1 Gainsford Place, in London's then fashionable Islington. They were J. R. and J. W. Barfoot.

Although they did not actually sign the puzzles, they always included pink roses in the pictures, often in the unlikeliest of places: between the paving stones of Ramsgate Harbour, and around the feet of an ugly rhino. On only one puzzle, *The Homes of England*, is there a signature combined with the pink roses that gave the game away over a century later.

Identical roses appear on a set of building bricks signed J. R. B. and J. W. B., and it was these initials that led (by way of some special natural history lithographs by J. R. Barfoot that had been

Four German puzzles published by Johann Trautner, Nuremberg c. 1800. These early examples of hand die-stamp cutting have characteristically interlocking pieces.

sold by the Holborn Hill Dartons in the 1840s) to the Royal Academy, which provided the Islington address. Both Barfoots were artists. J. R. was a miniaturist and his work was shown at the Academy for several years. J. W. was clearly very talented for his first picture was hung there in 1852 when he was fourteen years old.

It seems incredible now that they should have been determined to remain anonymous, but each euphemistically described himself in the 1851 census as 'Designer in Wood and Lithographic Artist'

and their workshop was carefully hidden behind high, solid brick walls in the garden of Gainsford Place. One likeness of J. W. Barfoot survives, the only portrait of an early jigsaw manufacturer; it is the size of a postage stamp and is signed 'Yours very sincerely J. W. B.'.

The late nineteenth century saw the full flowering of jigsaw puzzles. In Germany and Austria, where dissected maps had been imported from England for almost one hundred years, manufacturers cut romanticized childhood and classical scenes into tiny interlocking pieces. Their sophisticated cutting was possible because they used extremely thin wood – almost a veneer – backed with paper; and as they rarely used maps, they were not sidetracked into cutting large, simple pieces like those of the English puzzles. The most important manufacturer, and one of the first in the field, was the Viennese firm of Trentsensky. It specialized in all kinds of printed toys, from scrap sheets to toy theatres, and by the early nineteenth century dominated the puzzle-market in Austria and Southern Germany. Nuremberg, renowned for toy-manufacturing, had a few firms making puzzles, as did some other towns, but never in large quantities.

The skill of these manufacturers was far superior to that of the English, but they never caught the imagination of German-speaking Europe. A great many puzzles were, however, made for export, usually captioned in German, French and English. Almost all old puzzles found in Scandinavia, for example, are of German manufacture.

The French also used very thin wood, but did not take advantage of it for fine cutting. Like the Germans they cut interlocking pieces which bore no relation to the picture, but theirs were much larger. They sold the puzzles already made up, in sets of four or five, on stiff card, stacked one above the other. Some were made for export and captioned in several languages, including Spanish.

A toy historian, Henry René d'Allemagne, made an extraordinary claim in the catalogue of the 1900 Paris International Exhibition. He stated that the French had invented jigsaw puzzles in 1812, and then repeated the assertion six years later in his book *Recréations et Passe-Temps*. Puzzles were not as popular or well-known in France as they had become in England, which may explain d'Allemagne's ignorance of English puzzles

Row Boat Excursion. S. Wagner, Philadelphia 1860. A very early American-made puzzle, cut on a traditional European plan.

and indeed of the French dissected maps of the 1780s (two, one of France and one of Europe, had been engraved by Janvier and sold in 1786 by Lattré). But it was not only d'Allemagne who missed them; in 1807, George Bernard Depping, a German historian living in Paris, felt it was necessary to describe puzzles in great detail in his book *Les Soirées d'hiver* as though they were little known. By 1830, however, they had acquired their name of *jeux de patience*.

Puzzles from several European countries had been imported into the United States by the early nineteenth century. An advertisement placed in the *New York Advertiser* on 27 December 1823 by F. and R. Lockwood of 154 Broadway offered three geographical race games and ten different dissected maps, a long list of other didactic pastimes and 'Dissected Pictures – a great variety'. But it was not until 1850 that the first American-produced puzzle appeared. It was called *McCleary & Pierce's Geographical Analysis of the State of New York*, and was similar to the traditional English puzzles. In 1860, however, S. Wagner of Philadelphia published *Row Boat Excursion*, a hand-coloured lithograph dissected in the German manner into small interlocking pieces, and sold it fully made up in a box. Mr Wagner was clearly a recent arrival from the Old World; but his puzzle set no fashion. The American manufacturers followed the British style, cutting large pieces and packing their puzzles higgledy-piggledy.

Le jeu de patience.

Although the successful Americans followed the British in some ways they very soon added their own spice of originality. Arriving comparatively late on the puzzle scene, they were not inhibited by time-honoured conventions. Cardboard had been cheaply produced since the middle of the nineteenth century but English puzzle manufacturers had ignored it, continuing to make expensive hand-cut wooden puzzles. The Americans, however, seized on the new, cheap material and cut it in the most

Box lid of *Sliced Animals*. Selchow & Richter c.1900.

economical way – sliced in straight lines – with a guillotine. Slicing in its most basic form was shown in a puzzle made by the New York firm of Selchow & Richter (the inventors of *Scrabble*) called *Sliced Animals improved, or Spelling made Easy*. This consisted of parallel cardboard strips showing animal names and pictures for the child to put together.

Slicing had been used by European toy-makers, but not as a cheap alternative to dissected puzzles. They used the technique for wooden *Changeables*, sets of portraits sliced into three horizontally, to be assembled into different portraits. Rudolph Ackerman had published *Changeable Gentlemen* in London in 1819 and this was followed by *Changeable Ladies*. Ackerman is well known for establishing hand-coloured lithography as a fine art in England, but his arithmetic was deplorable; he announced

that from the twenty-eight changeable gentlemen 'upward of 5,000 portraits can be made' but from the same number of ladies 'the astonishing number of 21,952'. Other publishers adopted the idea, slicing long, coloured aquatint landscapes, into vertical parallel strips, which could be assembled in any order. An early version designed by a Mr Clarke was called *The Myriorama*; he claimed that 20,922,789,000 variations could be made and that 'if a person were occupied night and day, making one change every minute, he would not finish the task in less than 39,807,438 years and 330 days.' Clarke gave credit for the idea to Monsieur Bres of Paris, 'but his efforts, though very ingenious, partook of the imperfections incident to all first attempts.'

The Germans took the lead with all kinds of metamorphic puzzles, consisting of sliced-up humans and animals which could be made into fabulous creatures, primarily for the export market. *Metamorphosis Without End*, for example, is captioned in five languages and probably found its way to America.

From the 1860s onwards two of the most important American puzzle-makers were Milton Bradley & Company of Springfield, Massachusetts, and McLoughlin Brothers of New York, who were eventually absorbed by the former. Milton Bradley had considerable flair which, combined with the new techniques, inspired such ideas as *The Model Ship Puzzle*. This was a detailed picture of a fully-rigged sailing ship, with the name of each part – capstan, forebrace, flying bridge stay – incorporated in the design. These names were stamped out from the cardboard picture in small circular pieces. The rest was sliced into large pieces, each of which was itself sliced into several angular – not necessarily rectangular – pieces. For about half the cost, Bradley had produced a puzzle whose popularity would rival that of any made on the other side of the Atlantic. He followed it with another very successful one, *The Smashed-Up Locomotive : A Mechanical Puzzle for Boys*. The box lid showed a glorious, crashed engine, challenging any small boy to turn the muddled pieces into a complete, shining locomotive.

When it came to maps, however, Bradley followed Spilsbury's original idea. They were mounted on wood and dissected along the boundaries, and were often double-sided with a vivid picture of American activities on the back. Bradley's company continued the old tradition and even in their 1938 catalogue listed 'Dissected Maps: All cut on State Lines'. McLoughlin Brothers, on the other hand, produced cardboard maps cheerfully sliced up with no regard to the boundaries. Another of their cheap, sliced puzzles was a two-picture one called *Chopped Up Niggers*, with an illustration of a Negro dandy orator on one side and a minstrel version of Hamlet contemplating Yorick's skull on the other.

The House that Jack Built. C.C. Shepherd 1881. An early example of American ingenuity in using puzzles as the basis for games.

Bradley showed far more sensitivity in his wooden jigsaws, particularly in a set called *Diamonds and Toads* that was based on Kate Greenaway's children's book illustrations, first published in London in 1871.

C. C. Shepherd of New York, who provided conventional school equipment, lightened his own and his customers' lives by inventing *The House that Jack Built : A Picture Game*. The game began with an ordinary puzzle of Jack's house; once that was built, it was filled with characters from the nursery rhyme, provided on ten numbered cards.

There was a short-lived fashion at the end of the century for toy-book and puzzle packages, sold in handsome wooden boxes with gaily coloured sliding lids. They were sold by Raphael Tuck in London, and E. P. Dutton in New York. The puzzles were crudely coloured and coarsely cut, with subjects ranging from fairy tales to bible stories; they were usually double-sided and often showed two scenes on each side. Packed with them were picture books, sometimes comprising only key pictures to the puzzles, but sometimes showing several extra incidents in the hero's life. The pictures were chromolithographed in the great printing centre of Bavaria. Chromolithography had been used for children's books on both sides of the Atlantic for some years, but it had been too expensive for commercial puzzle-makers.

Another new development in puzzle-manufacture at that time was the cutting die. Instead of having each puzzle individually cut with a hand or mechanical saw, the manufacturers had dies made to cut large runs of puzzles at once. Dies are made from blocks of hardwood which are cut into the required number of pieces with a jig saw. Sharp steel rules are then bent to fit between the pieces and the blocks reassembled round them, leaving the sharp edges protruding above the wood. The blocks are then locked into place

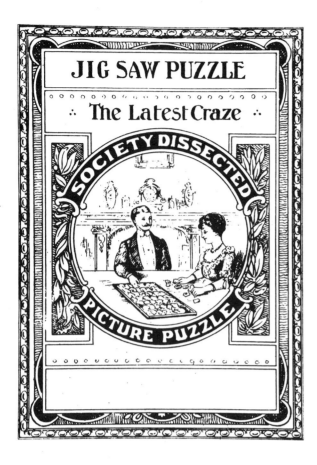

rather than cheap cardboard. Raphael Tuck, however, foresaw the possibilities of a new invention – plywood – and exploited it for incredibly complicated puzzles designed to absorb the attention of newly leisured adults. By 1914 the company had produced a 1,250-piece challenge called *The House of Lords.*

Raphael Tuck is best-known now for greetings cards, but at that time the company specialized in postcards, of which it held 60,000 different designs. During the early 1920s its two most profitable operations were combined in 'Puzzle Postcards'. Made from light cardboard and enclosed in a sealed folder with perforated edges, they could be addressed and sent anywhere in the world; all the recipient had to do was tear along the perforations to remove the made-up jigsaw. The puzzles' success was immense, and Tuck took out world patents to protect them. Soon he decided to sell them in packets of six, still postable, but primarily for use as 'Picture Puzzle Postcards for Progressive Puzzle Parties'. Printed score sheets were included in the pack and each player was supposed to record the time taken to complete one puzzle before progressing to the next. Tuck suggested that they could be made more difficult by mixing the pieces from two – or all six – puzzles before the party began.

'Picture Puzzle playing has caught on and is becoming a formidable rival of Bridge' announced an English weekly called *Truth. The Times* noted the new trend with its customary quiet

Right: Raphael Tuck puzzles – top: *Tuck's Zag-Zaw c.* 1910 (one of the earliest puzzles to be made from a photographic print); bottom: *Picture Puzzle Postcards for Progressive Puzzle Parties c.* 1920.

Below: *Punch* 9 March 1910.

WHAT IF THE JIG-SAW EPIDEMIC SPREADS?

to be used to stamp out the pieces of any number of different puzzles of the appropriate sizes. The puzzles themselves were no longer known as 'dissected puzzles'; although some firms experimented with the terms 'Zig-Saw' and 'Zag-Zaw', 'Jigsaw' was the name that, by the beginning of the twentieth century, had come into general use.

By then virtually every subject imaginable had been used for puzzles in England and the United States. Nursery rhymes were commonplace, as were industrial scenes, farms, alphabets and the traditional maps. In England many new publishers joined the race to provide novelties for a puzzle-mad public, but none as successfully as Raphael Tuck.

It was Tuck who propelled jigsaws into the adult market, and precipitated one of the wildest crazes in the history of puzzling. His company had started as art dealers, based in London with branches in Paris and New York, but it began making puzzles in 1890. With Sir Arthur Conan Doyle on the board, it increased its output with astonishing speed. Rapidly improving chromolithography had ousted the labour-intensive hand-colouring of puzzles, but they were still made of wood

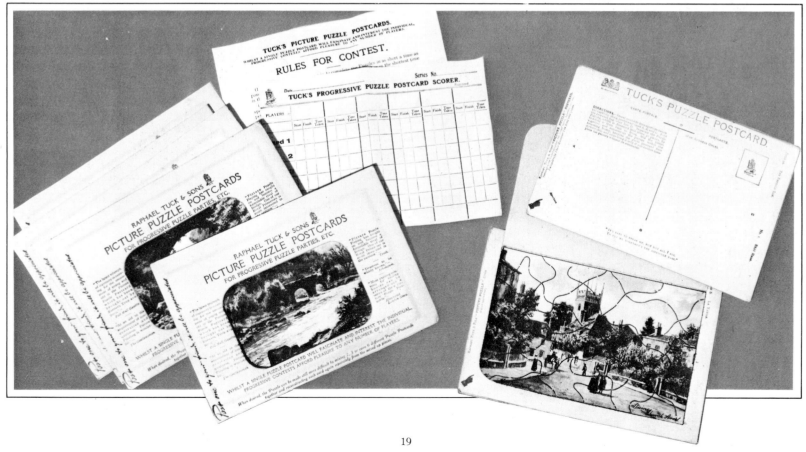

The Home of Washington – Mt. Vernon. Parker Brothers c.1930. A puzzle of superb quality from the 'Pastime Series'.

restraint, while *The Gentlewoman* was gushingly enthusiastic: 'One of the most absorbing and alluring games that has ever captured society. Boredom is a thing of the past in Belgravia since the art of puzzling.'

The same fever spread all over the United States, where it was later described as 'the country-wide craze for cardboard picture puzzles which nearly unhinged the national mind'. At one time over two million puzzles were sold every week. Many of these would have come from Parker Brothers, later called 'The Tiffany of the Games Business'. They had had great success with several games since about 1880; in 1909, realizing the potential of the adult puzzle market, they began cutting jigsaws from excellent reproductions of Old Masters and modern Kodachromes, mounted on plywood. The demand became overwhelming; as a result they had to stop production of all other games at their big plant at Salem. Their 'Pastime Puzzles', made from good-quality materials and deceptively simple, took the puzzle world by storm. Like Raphael Tuck, Parker Brothers included all kinds of shapes in the cutting of their jigsaws – animals, tools, arms, legs and so on – but they also included all kinds of tricks which made the puzzles immensely difficult to do; the cuts would follow the edge of a colour or pattern so that there were no clues to help in putting it together, and straight edges would be used within the puzzle to confuse the puzzler. Even the 350-piece *Mount Vernon, the Home of Washington* was a patience-trier, owing to its subtle cutting. The fame and popularity of 'Pastime Puzzles' spread far

beyond America and in the 1920s and '30s they were sent overseas in huge numbers.

If Parker Brothers were the Tiffany of the games business, then Frank Ware was the Rolls-Royce of puzzle-makers. He started making jigsaws with John Henriques during the Great Depression when the USA's thousands of jobless looked to puzzles to kill their endless time. Many others tried their hands at jigsaw-manufacture, but Ware and Henriques went on to develop the world's most exclusive custom trade in jigsaws, with puzzles costing anything up to $2,000. They mounted silk-screen printed pictures on five-ply mahogany, cut them into fiendishly complicated shapes, and packed them in plain black boxes. One of their trade-marks was a seahorse shape that was cut into every puzzle. Special shapes could also be cut on demand. Ware and Henriques did everything possible to complicate and confuse: on the box lid they would print a misleading title, for example *Kid in a Can* for a knight in armour. They would also specify a 'par time' – that is, the length of time Henriques considered necessary to complete the puzzle. Customers who could not complete the puzzle in time were considered not 'up to par'; this must have proved quite a challenge to the Rockefellers, Du Ponts and Vanderbilts, whose requests filled the company's order books. Even the Duke and Duchess of Windsor commissioned 'Par Puzzles'.

The Duke's jigsaws always had pieces in the shape of his four Cairn terriers incorporated in the cutting, while the Duchess insisted on her initials W.W. One 'Par Puzzle', possibly the

Below: *The Contest*. Par Puzzles. The par time for this puzzle is 5 hours 20 minutes.

Right: some of its pieces, showing the exquisitely fine cutting. The seahorse shape is the trademark of Par Puzzles.

biggest jigsaw made at that time, consisted of 10,000 pieces. Irregularly shaped, with no straight edges anywhere, it was so difficult that even Henriques could not put a par time to it; he just called it *Days and Nights*. When Frank Ware retired a few years ago he gave his stock, goodwill and the name 'Par Puzzles' to Arthur Gallagher, whose son is still hand-cutting complicated jigsaws in New York State today.

It was not only in America that the Depression and its attendant unemployment caused an increased demand for jigsaw puzzles. In Britain Frederick Warne, publishers of all kinds of children's books, found book sales falling off but managed to keep every one of their staff by switching some to their successful jigsaw-puzzle department. One of their authors was Beatrix Potter, whose drawings of endearing animal characters made very popular puzzles. When the bad times were over, the staff returned to book publishing; none the less, over fifty years later, Warne's are still making and selling Beatrix Potter's *Tom Kitten* jigsaw, although the modern standard die-cut has made the puzzle much easier and quicker to assemble than the original version.

Since then puzzles have never had quite the crazy popularity they enjoyed in the 1930s, but groups of dedicated adult puzzlers have, at different times, banded together to form clubs. One of the first was organized by a Brighton bookshop about sixty years ago. Once a week the owners sent out puzzles to all their members. Pasted on the lid of each box was a menacing label, exhorting the borrower to record the return date and any missing pieces; one large puzzle was borrowed twenty-eight times between 27 April 1929 and 16 December 1930 without a single piece being lost. Frank Ware and John Henriques also ran a club

The Traveller's Problem Puzzle. Einson-Freeman *c.* 1920. One of a series of 25-cent, cardboard mystery puzzles, for which clues to the solution were printed on the box.

An early *Double-Decker* puzzle published by Chad Valley. These are especially difficult in that they have to be correctly assembled in three dimensions.

for a while, but the organization took up so much of their time that they closed it down. Milton Bradley, who understood the wear and tear on library puzzles, announced: 'For circulating libraries ... picture puzzles may be obtained in cloth-covered, reinforced boxes of great durability which will stand indefinitely the hard usage to which rental puzzles are subjected.'

Clubs and libraries may cater for select groups of dedicated puzzlers (today in Herefordshire there is a flourishing postal club whose members have a choice of over 4,000 puzzles), but with the introduction of cardboard and die-cutting, jigsaws became and have remained a recreation for the masses. Although vast numbers of inexpensive, mass-produced puzzles are now available, the subject matter for adults is limited, in the main, to reproductions of well-known paintings and photographic views of famous beauty spots.

Specialist and small companies, however, have used every kind of subject at every level of sophistication, including the first nude to appear in *The Sunday Times*. Devised by a young marketing expert, this young lady figured on both sides of an amusing cardboard puzzle sold in a box marked '*Private and Confidential* – for adult eyes only'. Inside, the girl is shown putting the last piece into a jigsaw of another famous nude – Michelangelo's 'David'.

Recently the publisher Harry N. Abrams of New York used an anamorphic portrait of Charles II for a fascinating circular puzzle. He provided a flexible metallic card which, correctly placed in the centre of the completed puzzle, reflected the King undistorted. But the ultimate in brain-teasing is the plain white puzzle that has appeared at different times during this century. Some manufacturers suggest that the puzzler draws his own picture on its blank surface, but real addicts make it up as it is.

Many jigsaw fanatics are crossword puzzlers too, and in 1979 Onsworld Limited published a package consisting of two black and white crossword jigsaw puzzles. They suggested alternative ways of solving these puzzles within puzzles: either by doing the crosswords first and using the completed answers to provide clues to the jigsaws, or by assembling the 2,000-piece jigsaws unaided and then filling in the crossword answers.

For people who want an exclusive puzzle, some manufacturers will still hand-cut puzzles with a message or a name incorporated in the cutting. Another expensive present for puzzle-addicts was recently devised by a silversmith, whose puzzles consist of small dissected rectangles of solid silver. Less extravagant individualists can have their own photographs mounted and die-cut into completely personal puzzles. And for those who prefer to do jigsaws standing up, an American company has devised a magnetic puzzle.

Novelists, playwrights and film directors have used jigsaw-puzzling to characterize obsessive and neurotic people, but some psychologists believe that puzzlers are always calm and sane. Springbok Editions in the United States made a puzzle called *Your Secret Self* for instant psycho-analysis. It consisted of 280 pieces made in eight different colours, each one fitting into every other. The final arrangement of colours gave clues to the puzzler's state of mental health, which could be assessed with the help of a booklet enclosed in the puzzle box.

An article published in America in 1909 describing the pleasures and pains of puzzling ends: 'The only man who can be perfectly happy about puzzle pictures is the man who makes them'. In 1975 such a man made one approximately 11×9 m cut into 1,020 pieces, breaking the record for the largest puzzle, though not for the one with the greatest number of pieces. That record is held by a jigsaw cut into about 40,000 pieces.

Jigsaw puzzles have come a long way from their beginnings in Spilsbury's shop two centuries ago. Perhaps the fascination they exert over puzzlers of every age and nationality has something to do with the timeless dream of creating order out of chaos.

Private and Confidential for adult eyes only. Tony Eccles 1969.
A double-sided, cardboard jigsaw puzzle.

THEMES AND VARIATIONS

I n 1798, Richard Lovell Edgeworth wrote in *Practical Education*: 'Whoever is used to children has seen that no toy is more permanently in requisition than dissected maps or pictures.' He was very well qualified to comment, having educated his own twenty-two children at home. They were all intelligent and the eldest, Maria, became a successful novelist. Her father believed that puzzles were perfect for assessing character: 'The child who quickly perceives resemblances catches instantly at the first bit of the wooden map that seems likely to answer his purpose: he makes perhaps twenty trials before he hits the right; whilst the wary youth cautiously examines with his eye the whole outline before his hand begins to move and, having exactly compared the two indentures, he joins them. He is slow but sure, and wins the day.' He strongly recommended puzzles for teaching geography to boys destined for the army or navy: 'It is surprising to see the constancy and patience, which the children show in putting them together, and the alacrity with which, day after day, they return to their work.'

A battered diary written in 1820 by the mother of six children echoes Edgeworth. A daily timetable was written out for the children's tutor, Mr Williams, under the general heading of 'Let all things be done in decency and order.' On Thursday afternoon, 'Fred and Emma, Ancient History, while Lucy puts a map together'; for another day, 'Horace, Geography with Dissected Map'; and once, 'should Fred and Emma know their lessons before the expiration of their half-hour, they may be employed putting maps together.'

Throughout the nineteenth century maps were the mainstay of teaching puzzles. The most prolific publisher was William Peacock, who used maps printed by established firms such as George Phillip. Peacock's puzzles were all colour-printed, accurate and unembellished; a few were double-sided with a colourful picture on the reverse, but, unlike the Barfoots, Peacock always gave priority to the map and dissected the board along the political boundaries. His output, which extended into the twentieth century, was prodigious and the majority of Victorian map puzzles extant today came from his factory. Milton Bradley's maps of the late 1930s were still dissected in the manner pioneered by Spilsbury, in spite of the widespread use of mechanical die-cutting for other puzzles.

Historical puzzles had a shorter life than maps, from 1780 to about 1900. They were almost all based on the same system of rows and rows of monarchs, but they became simpler and more attractive as the years passed. John Wallis offered an interesting alternative when he dissected a race game called *Historical Pastime of a New Game of the History of England*, which he had co-published in 1805. There were 157 oval portraits and scenes to each reign, and the race track progressed chronologically from the outside to George III at the centre of the spiral. Once the track was assembled it became a kind of *Snakes and Ladders*, each player moving round the spiral at the throw of a die; if a player landed on poor, beheaded Mary, Queen of Scots he was sent back

Kings and Queens of England.
Edward Wallis c. 1835. Boxed pieces.

NEW GAME OF THE HISTORY OF ENGLAND
John Harris and John Wallis 1803.

to the beginning, and Shakespeare cost two counters unless the player could recite two consecutive lines from one of his plays; Henry VIII was a good place to fall, because that player could collect all the fines on the pretext of plundering Thomas à Becket's tomb. Another attractive exception was devised by William Sallis soon after Queen Victoria's accession. Imaginative but inexperienced, Sallis was not trapped by puzzle-makers' conventions; by profession he was a book-binder and manufacturer of cards and pattern books, and he devised a puzzle entitled *The Child's Picture History of England* which was triangular, the young Queen taking pride of place at the apex.

Almost the longest-running subject for didactic puzzles has been the alphabet. Around 1790 William Darton brought out *Miscellanies for the Instruction of Infants*, a heavy-sounding puzzle which was in fact based on the familiar 'A is for Apple'; its only strange feature was the rhyme for Z, which posed a problem before zoos and zebra were brought to London: 'In Scripture Zebulon we find, to be a fisher man inclin'd.' Darton's alphabet puzzle was followed by others: alphabets of animals and flags, and a particularly attractive alphabet village.

After about 1810 multiplication puzzles began to appear. Like dates, tables were tedious to learn by rote, but could be fun if they were incorporated in a puzzle. Wallis and Darton, whose puzzles were expensive, thought the idea through more carefully

Box lid c. 1820. This is the earliest known picture of children doing a puzzle.

than did the anonymous, more down-market firms. The latter printed 'twice two are four' on one piece whereas the more established manufacturers had 'twice two' on one piece and 'are four' on the next. But all of them decked out the pieces with colourful pictures to lighten their victims' task. Their successors

are still making arithmetical puzzles for very young children.

Teachers even tried to sweeten the rules of grammar in the 1820s. Several books had been published with titles such as *The Infants' Grammar or a Picnic Party of the Parts of Speech*; they were followed in 1830 by a puzzle, *A Picturesque Grammar of the English Language, by Dr. Syntax*, showing charming everyday

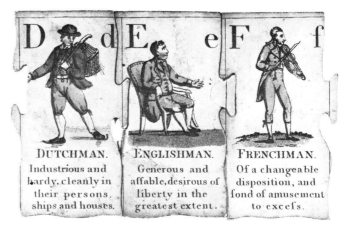

Pieces from *Inhabitants of the World*. William Darton c. 1790. Hand-coloured engraving of men of twenty-six nationalities used for an original alphabet puzzle.

scenes to explain the use of conjunctions, interjections and other dreary but vital matters.

Less formal subjects have also been used to make educational puzzles. Most children are naturally curious, continually asking questions about how and why things are made, and puzzle-manufacturers have been quick to satisfy the needs of distracted parents unable to give the right answers. All kinds of industrial processes have been explained, from the manufacture of Royal Worcester porcelain to the stages through which tea and coffee must pass between harvesting and drinking. Some designers have combined several industries in the same puzzle and others, like John Betts, have included explanatory booklets.

The first part of the twentieth century saw a decline in the popularity of didactic puzzles, although alphabets, multiplication tables and 'how-to' pictures have continued to be used intermittently. In recent years clock puzzles have been published to teach children how to tell the time, and there have even been telephone-dialling jigsaws, to explain another necessity of modern life. Now that child psychologists have recognized the educational value of play, enlightened parents take their children's jigsaws very seriously, secure in the knowledge that puzzles teach tiny children spatial co-ordination, judgement and observation, among other invaluable skills. If he were alive today, Richard Lovell Edgeworth would find himself among many kindred spirits.

SCIENCE IN SPORT, OR THE PLEASURES OF NATURAL PHILOSOPHY
A dissected table game to be played with counters and a teetotum. John Wallis 1805.

MISCELLANIES FOR THE INSTRUCTION OF INFANTS
Probably the earliest example of an alphabet jigsaw puzzle.
William Darton c. 1790.

LADDER OF LEARNING
This shows a gentler approach to the same subject. The swags of roses
identify the anonymous artist. J. W. Barfoot c. 1855.

CHRONOLOGICAL TABLES OF THE HISTORY OF FRANCE,
FROM PHARAMOND THE FIRST KING TO THE REIGN OF LEWIS XVI
Newbury and Wallis 1791.

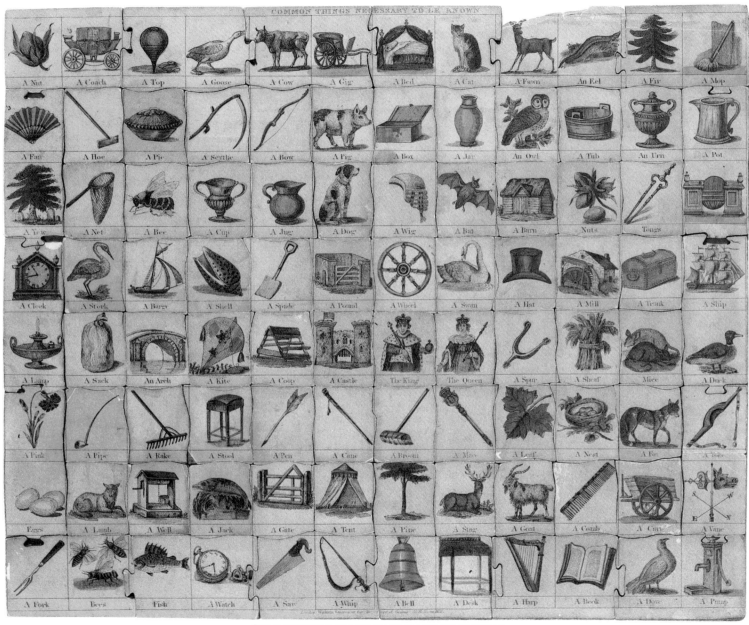

COMMON THINGS NECESSARY TO BE KNOWN
Ninety-six hand-coloured woodcuts of named objects, probably
used as a spelling aid. William Darton *c.* 1825.

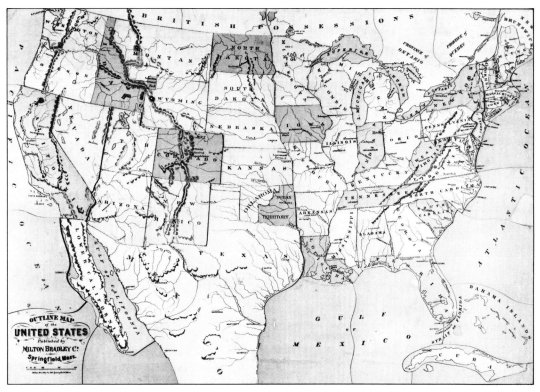

OUTLINE MAP OF THE UNITED STATES
A double-sided map, cut to the state boundaries, showing scenes from American life
on the reverse. Milton Bradley. Probably 1870s.

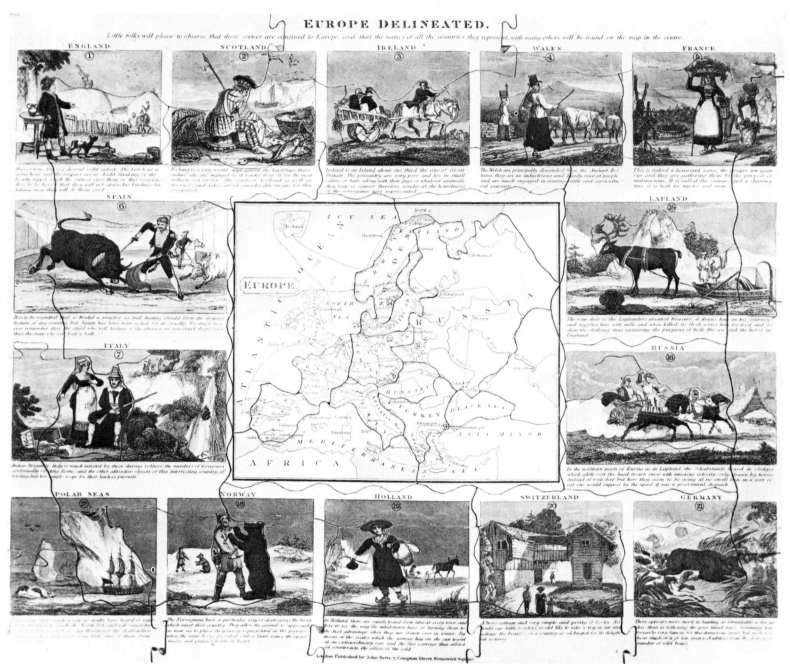

EUROPE DELINEATED

Also a geographical game, this was advertised by Betts as 'a Series of
engravings on Steel, tastily coloured'. John Betts 1830.

35

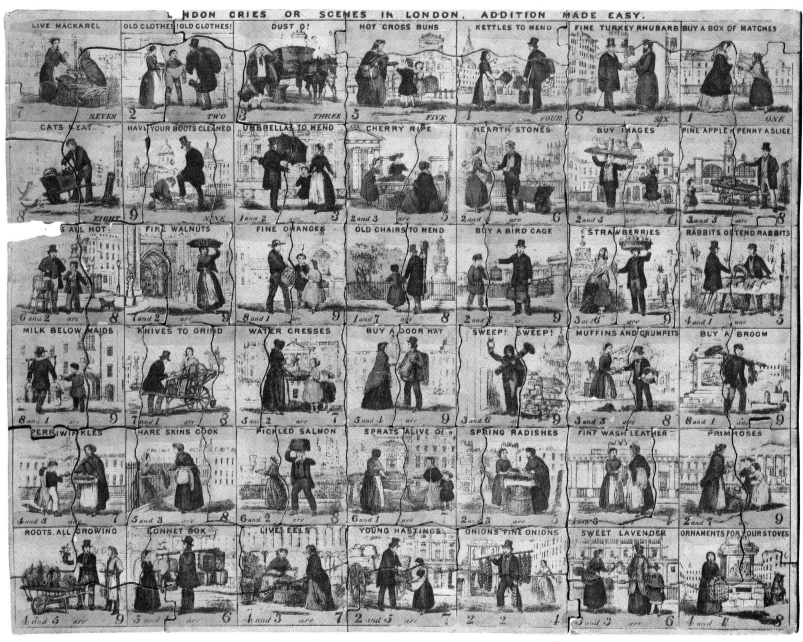

LONDON CRIES, OR SCENES IN LONDON. ADDITION MADE EASY
Each of the forty-two traders shown in the puzzle is posed
against an identifiable London building *c.* 1860.

PROVINCES OF FRANCE
One of a set of three French puzzles from the late nineteenth century,
showing the regions of the country.

David Slaying the Lion. Religious Tract Society *c.* 1855.

The Transgressor Miracle Play c. 1930.

Although the Victorian era was the heyday of moral instruction of children, some puzzle manufacturers had designed religious and moralistic puzzles even earlier, in the late eighteenth century. William Darton made one in 1789, urging children to love virtue and abhor vice. His message was eye-catchingly illustrated with a pair of trees, one with its fruit of evil hanging on bare branches, the other with glowing red fruits of goodness hanging in luxuriant foliage. Judging by the worn condition of remaining examples of this puzzle, it was very popular. Unfortunately it heralded a mere decade of imaginative moral puzzles, which were then superseded by a more rigid style.

In most Victorian households children were forbidden toys on Sundays, but biblical and moral puzzles did not count as games and were therefore permitted. A character in one of Mrs Molesworth's children's stories spelt it out: 'You may have your Biblical dissections on Sundays, and your other other puzzles during the Christmas holidays.' Several of the Sunday dissections were made from rebus puzzles, in which small pictures were substituted for particular words in a text. *The Creed, The Lord's Prayer* and *The Ten Commandments* were popular titles, as was Benjamin Franklin's *Poor Richard*, a homily on the virtues of diligence and frugality. *Poor Richard* had had great success on both sides of the Atlantic, and was published in various pirated editions before the puzzle-makers adapted it.

Another very popular book at the time was John Bunyan's *Pilgrim's Progress*, which inspired generations of puzzle-makers between 1790 and 1870. Some manufacturers reproduced scenes described by Bunyan, while others merely borrowed his ideas.

A child's attention could have been caught by any of these pictorial puzzles, but the serried ranks of biblical characters in *Key to the Old Testament* were as difficult and dull as the early historical tables of kings had been. It soon dawned on manufacturers, however, that the Bible contained some highly exciting stories which would make admirable dissections. The early versions were a little stiff, but by the 1850s they had become relaxed, colourful and very popular. Scenes such as Daniel in the Lions' Den and Pharaoh drowning in the Red Sea were used on their own by some companies, while others combined pictures of several incidents in one puzzle.

In the early years of this century, once Sunday schools had removed the onus of providing religious education from harassed parents, the popularity of religious puzzles died. Today's children are not subjected to such delights as *Timely Cautions* and *Grandmama Goodsoul's Scripture Alphabet*, in the hope that the pictured examples will instil in them virtue and moral fibre, and their Sundays are their own.

THE HILL OF SCIENCE, AN ALLEGORY
John Wallis 1807.

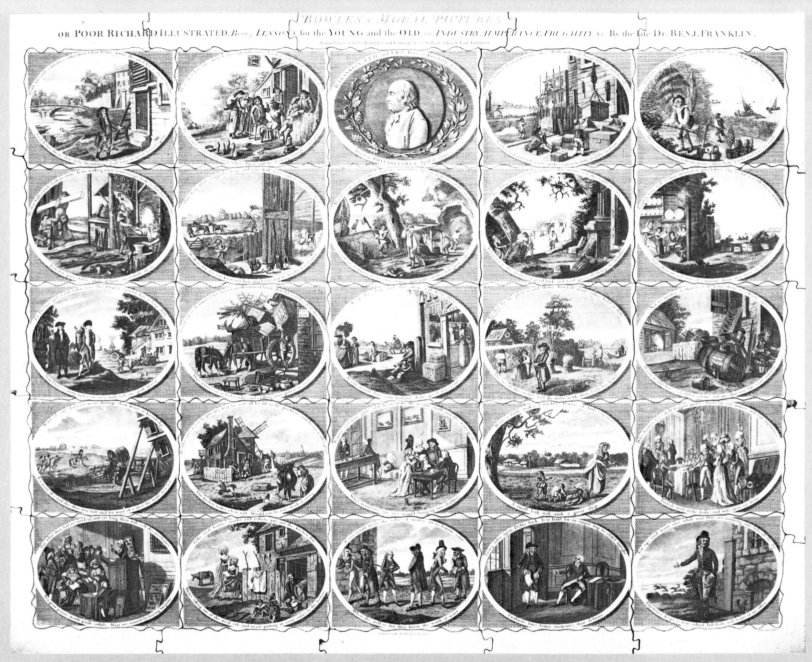

BOWLES'S MORAL PICTURES, OR POOR RICHARD ILLUSTRATED
One of the many puzzles based on Benjamin Franklin's *Poor Richard*.
Bowles and Carver 1795.

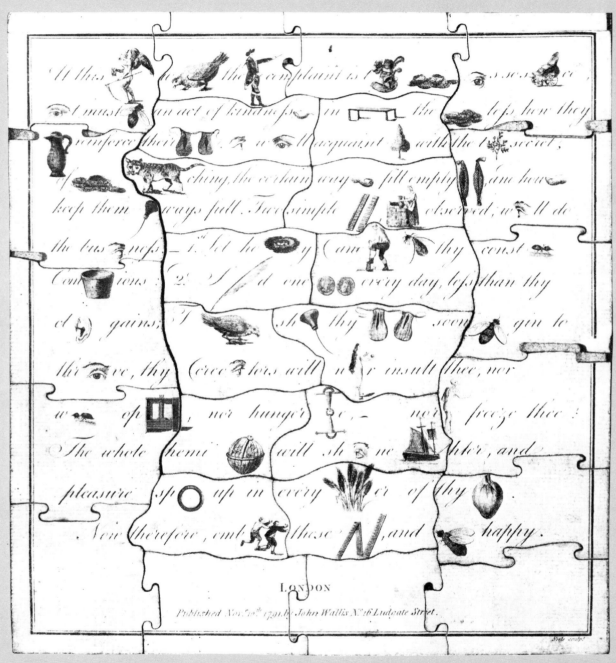

REBUS
Another puzzle based on Benjamin Franklin's book.
John Wallis 1791.

"AND ADAM GAVE NAMES TO ALL CATTLE, AND TO THE FOWL OF THE AIR, AND TO EVERY BEAST OF THE FIELD."

SCRIPTURE, NATURAL HISTORY & ZOOLOGY
Hand-coloured engraving of Adam naming the beasts, captioned with
a quotation from the *Book of Genesis*. Edward Wallis 1838.

PICTURES FROM THE BIBLE, A PUZZLE BOX FOR LITTLE ONES
A set of puzzles cut from colour lithographs on card; printed in Bavaria.
Ernest Nister, London and E. P. Dutton, New York c. 1910.

The Farm. John Wallis 1812. This puzzle cost 5 shillings in 1814.

The Romantic poets' attitude to 'the calm that Nature breathes among the hills and groves' was reflected in late eighteenth- and very early nineteenth-century natural history puzzles. By 1810, however, idealized pastoral scenes began to give way to more realistic pictures of the natural world. John Wallis published an instructive puzzle in 1812 called *The Farm*, an animated farmyard scene featuring men and women hard at work on their allotted tasks. Other puzzle-makers followed his lead, and in 1845 John Betts made *My Uncle's Farm*. This was typical of his technique and showed twenty-one small farm scenes, each with a number referring to the accompanying booklet. Betts could never resist these solemn little books, which he included with biblical, historical and industrial puzzles alike.

As the century progressed the Barfoots' influence succeeded in softening the attitude to farming without sentimentalizing it. Their single-scene puzzles of *Sheep Shearing* and *Harvest Home* are charming pictures garlanded with the characteristic pink roses.

The Barfoots were also well ahead of their time in that they stressed the animals' role in the farming world in a puzzle they called *Kindness to Animals*. All young children love animals, therefore it is not surprising that puzzle-makers have so often featured them. Small travelling menageries, not uncommon early in the century, provided the inspiration for several colourful puzzles featuring exotic creatures, the first of which was *Walker's New Menagerie* in 1810. The real fillip came, however, in 1828

with the opening of London's Zoological Gardens. The Wallises, the Dartons and a host of others began choosing suitable prints to dissect. The best one was probably Edward Wallis's *A New View of the Zoological Gardens*, published in 1835. As well as the key picture it included useful information about the price and conditions of admission (a shilling – 5p – as opposed to over £2 today), and a review of the animals on show: monkeys 'whose antics and burlesque imitations of the human race excite the laughter of spectators', and the elephant who 'is surprising to watch in his various motions of eating, drinking, bathing, walking etc.'

After a few years, delight in strange and exotic creatures was superseded by the typically Victorian attitudes illustrated in such down-to-earth puzzles as *Domestic Animals and their Uses : The Cow* and *Graphic Illustrations of Animals Showing their Utility to Man : The Horse*. The cow was shown to produce milk, butter, cheese, boots, harness leather and strings for musical instruments.

While domestic animals were being assessed, the whole animal kingdom was tabulated in a puzzle called *Zoology of the Earth's Four Quarters, Panoramically arranged, with the likeness of nearly*

Box lid of *The Comparative Size of Forty Birds, From the Ostrich to the Humming Bird*. N. Carpenter *c*. 1835. A companion to *The Comparative Size of Thirty-Nine Animals* (p. 48)

1860s sentimentality was taking over. Children were encouraged to view animals indulgently – in, for example, pictures of a cock and hen surrounded by their brood of fluffy chicks, or a dog facing up to an angry goose. They were being led irrevocably to the real sentimentality that gushed out at the end of the nineteenth century and into the new. Pictures of sad-eyed puppies, kittens enmeshed in knitting wool and angelic children feeding birds were typical choices of turn-of-the-century puzzle-makers. An immense improvement on these were the Beatrix Potter puzzles, made by Frederick Warne, which have proved perennially successful.

Recently the teaching element has re-emerged in nature puzzles. John Waddington & Co., one of the largest modern manufacturers, have published series of natural-history puzzles with useful facts printed inside the boxes. Other modern puzzle-makers have returned to farmyard puzzles designed to teach very young children about domestic animals and their uses to man.

Romanticized landscapes have also reappeared. During the 1920s and '30s there were endless chocolate-box paintings of coaching scenes, bluebell woods and gambolling lambs to be cut into puzzles. Now, in the age of sophisticated photography, toyshops are lined with boxes displaying photographs of the Lake District, Anne Hathaway's Cottage, the Grand Canyon and famous beauty spots from all over the world. With package holidays to remote parts of the globe within the reach of most puzzle-addicts, manufacturers have to search for ever more exotic scenes to photograph.

A peacock from a set of five puzzles in *The Animals Puzzle Box*. Ernest Nister and E.P. Dutton. Printed in Bavaria c. 1910.

Right: cut-out puzzle of a cow. The maker is unknown but probably American; the cutting closely resembles that of *The House that Jack Built* (p. 17)

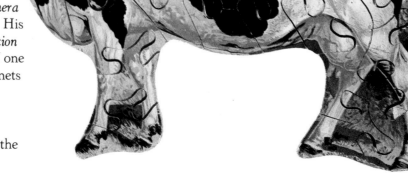

One Hundred Articulate Animals. Made from a very dull lithograph, it illustrated butterflies, moths, insects and crustaceans, all carefully described under their respective headings. William Edwards dissected *The Genera of Shells, Arranged According to the System of Linnaeus* in 1845. His puzzle was boxed with a small book called *A Familiar Introduction to Conchology*, but in spite of its forbidding name the puzzle is one of the most charming of the period. Edwards, who made cabinets for natural history specimens, also included an advertisement with *The Genera of Shells*, stating that he 'sold Amusing and Intellectual Toys', but none has survived.

He was one of the last to sell puzzles of this genre, and by the

A PRESENTATION OF THIRTY-SIX BIRDS COMMONLY SEEN IN ENGLAND
John Marshall 1821.

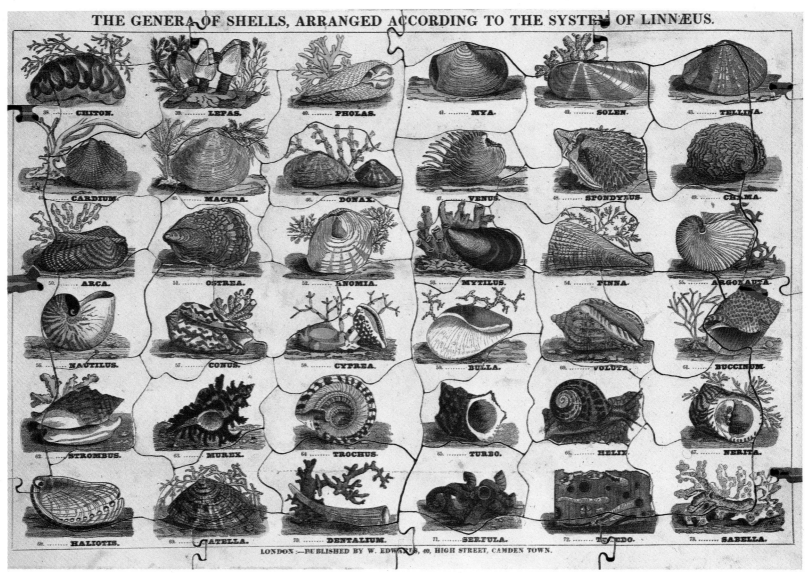

THE GENERA OF SHELLS, ARRANGED ACCORDING TO THE SYSTEM OF LINNÆUS
W. Edwards *c*. 1845.

THE COMPARATIVE SIZE OF THIRTY-NINE ANIMALS, FROM THE ELEPHANT TO THE MOUSE
N. Carpenter c. 1835.

A NEW VIEW OF THE ZOOLOGICAL GARDENS
The Zoological Gardens in Regent's Park, London were first
opened to the public in 1828. E. Wallis c. 1835.

THE LION'S COURT. THE TRIAL OF REYNARD THE FOX
One of Parker Brothers' famous 'Pastime Puzzles', it was sold in a
plain white box with no key picture.

FATHER TUCK'S PICTURE-BUILDING AT THE FARM
The puzzles are made of two layers of card, so that when an animal piece
is removed its name is revealed. Raphael Tuck *c*. 1909.

BIRD IN FLIGHT
Plywood puzzle in the shape of a bluebird. Holtzapffel, London *c*. 1910.

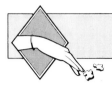

Launch of the Thunderer Man of War.

John Spilsbury's dissected maps were designed to teach children how the countries of the world fitted together, but after his death his successors' maps began to reflect the increasing mobility of the population. Coaches were better designed and faster – with a good team of horses it was possible to achieve the incredible speed of 16 mph – and at last something was being done to improve the post roads. *The Traveller's Companion, or the Post Roads of England and Wales with Distances Measured in Miles* was published in 1786, with a vigorous cartouche of a flying coach and four. Then John Wallis, who always went one better than everyone else, began to include the packet routes from England to France and Ireland, with other useful information: 'From Milford Haven to Waterford, 30 leagues, sailing every evening at 6 o'clock.'

In spite of this interest in travel at home and abroad, the vehicles of travel did not take the fancy of the dissectors until well into the nineteenth century. In 1831 an anonymous publisher produced *The Thunderer* to commemorate the launching of a massive 84-gun man-of-war. In spite of her sinister purpose, the ship was sent off on her maiden voyage with flags, cheers and royal smiles. *The Thunderer* was typical of many puzzles designed to commemorate a single occasion by small companies or individuals looking for a quick profit.

Nineteenth-century England took a great pride in the expansion of her Empire and her industries – both of which depended on efficient transport – and established puzzle-manufacturers took full advantage of this. An important one, John Betts, produced *The Dock-Yard, with the Ship in all its Stages*, a sober puzzle with an uncompromisingly didactic booklet. But few were as serious as that: *View of the Greenwich Rail Road Viaduct from Corbetts Lane*, again anonymously published, was typical of the more entertaining sort. The Greenwich railway line, opened in 1836, was considered to be the eighth wonder of the world because it had to pass over a high viaduct three miles long. To the irritation of the railway company the public, refusing to recognize it as a serious commercial undertaking, used it for joy-riding.

Other railway routes were taken up by the regular publishers, as were the great termini at Liverpool, Birmingham, Manchester and London. Edward Wallis made a detailed train puzzle, showing potential travellers exactly what comfort they could expect for different prices; a chilly open truck for third-class passengers contrasted with the covered compartments of the first class. This picture also proves that the modern idea of ferrying cars on long-distance trains is not a new one; with the horses

Box lid of a puzzle published by McLoughlin Brothers in 1901, showing 'the famous 999 New York Central Locomotive which set a world speed record'.

Above: *The Smashed-up Locomotive: A Mechanical Puzzle for Boys.* Milton Bradley *c.* 1875. An American puzzle showing the technique of slicing.

Below: *Balloon Ascent from Batty's Hippodrome c.* 1851.

safely stored in a horsebox, it was possible to travel in the stately comfort of a private carriage with a coachman on the box and footmen up behind.

The Americans had important ships and railways too, but showed their pride in more colourful puzzles than those of Betts and his colleagues. Milton Bradley's bright, brash *The*

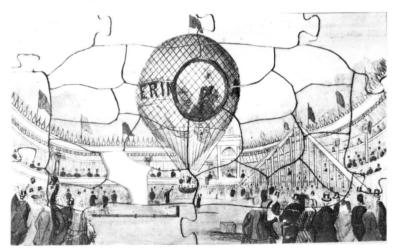

Smashed-Up Locomotive included a leaflet deploring children's (and even adults') ignorance of the names of engine parts and explaining that in the puzzle 'all the prominent parts have their names printed upon them and are cut out with one die, and hence are interchangeable'. It was up to the puzzlers to learn where the steam chest or smoke stack fitted, and they were given no help: the customary pattern or key picture was deliberately left out.

In the early 1920s Chad Valley, the toy manufacturers, began to make jigsaws in England. One of their successes was *The Schneider Cup Trophy* celebrating Britain's triumph in the famous air race. But the more leisurely travel of ocean-going liners and railways was their forte. They made the famous G.W.R. puzzles for the Great Western Railway, choosing pictures of historic towns, such as Windsor and Oxford, through which the line passed. They cut a splendid double puzzle of Paddington Station as seen by Frith in 1862 and 'today' in 1928, and others of famous express trains and engines such as 'King George V'. The puzzles were available at all Great Western stations, as well as toyshops, and at one time the railway company claimed to have sold over 200,000. Very young travellers could buy a jigsaw depicting an engine mounted on runners.

People bought Great Western Railway puzzles not only as souvenirs, but also to assemble during long journeys. The *Daily*

The Photo Picture Puzzle. Davidson Brothers. London and New York *c*.1910. Showing 'Cody's Airship', this is one of the early photographic jigsaw puzzles.

Mail reported in 1924 that: 'In passing through Pullman Cars on a journey, one is likely to find half the travellers working at the Puzzles, and at mealtimes there are notices, "please do not touch", on partly completed Puzzles all through the trains. Similar notices are to be found in the Saloons of Atlantic liners.' Puzzles were certainly part of the shipboard routine, and ships' shops always stocked large selections.

One of the longest puzzles then made was the *Twilight Express* designed by Milton Bradley and described in the 1931 catalogue: 'A complete train, comprising locomotive, baggage car, Pullman sleeping car, dining car and observation car. The locomotive is of

Traffic on the Road. Spears Games *c*.1930.

the most approved type used by the New York Central System for the Empire State Express and other fast trains, and the cars are faithfully reproduced in colours from photographs supplied by the Pullman Company. These parts when put together form a train over nine feet long, with a scenic background which adds to its attractiveness.'

The period between the World Wars was one of record-breaking, and jigsaw manufacturers watched avidly for suitable subjects. Campbell's *Blue Bird* was used, as was the *Yankee Clipper Flying Boat*, which successfully completed her long-distance maiden flight from Baltimore to Southampton and back just before the Second World War.

In the 1960s and '70s the development of space research inspired many puzzles of rockets, launching pads and journeys in

The Yankee Clipper Flying Boat. Williams, Ellis & Co. 1939. From a series of puzzles celebrating twelve 'wonders of the world'.

outer space. On a more earthly plane, London Transport has recently collaborated on a jigsaw map of the Underground featuring one of its bye-laws: 'The booking clerk may stop issuing puzzles for any train if this is necessary to avoid delaying the train.' The Paris Metro and the New York City subway system have also come under the jigsaw-makers' cutting dies, as has a picture of the Los Angeles freeways which are a puzzle in themselves.

Even if the pace of modern life precludes the sort of journeys where 'half the travellers can be found working at puzzles' it is clear that the links between travelling and puzzling that were forged in the eighteenth century are unlikely to be broken.

OFF TO THE HUNT
Publisher unknown *c.* 1920.

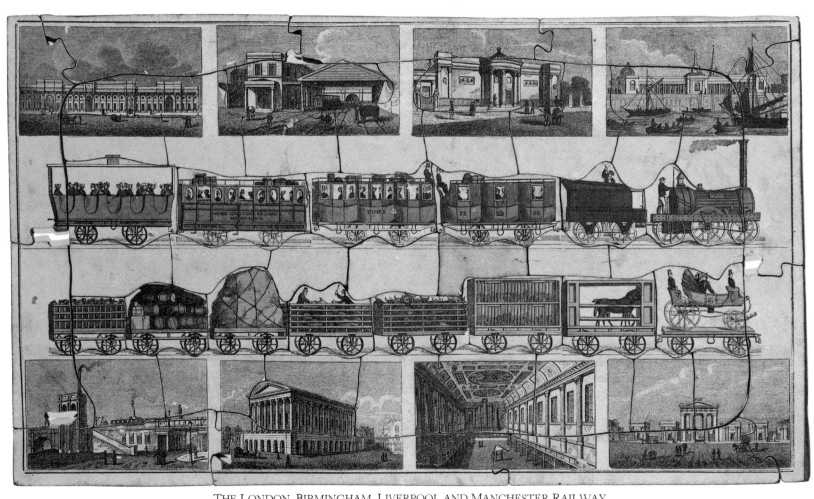

THE LONDON, BIRMINGHAM, LIVERPOOL AND MANCHESTER RAILWAY
Edward Wallis *c.* 1840.

THE GREAT WESTERN ST. BERNARD STEAM ENGINE

LOCOMOTIVES OLD AND NEW

THE RAILWAY STATION
Paddington Station as seen in 1862 by William Frith in his famous painting
The Railway Station and by a 'modern' painter half a century later. Made by Chad Valley Co.
and published by the Great Western Railway Company 1920s.

THE DOCK-YARD, WITH THE SHIP IN ALL ITS STAGES
A fine lithograph by John Gilbert. One of the best of
Betts's instructional puzzles, it was sold complete with a twenty-page
descriptive booklet for 5s. John Betts c. 1845.

61

LAUNCHING THE LIFEBOAT
Double-sided puzzle *c.* 1910.

THE MODEL SHIP
Milton Bradley *c.* 1875.

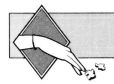

It is surprising that the most melancholy poet of his generation inspired the first fun jigsaw puzzle. Bullied at school, suicidal in youth, William Cowper enjoyed few happy years, but it was in one of these, 1782, that he wrote 'John Gilpin'. The ballad was first published anonymously in the *Public Advertiser*, but its appearance in an anthology printed in 1785 was

Key picture from *Johnny Gilpin of Cheapside*. John Wallis c.1783.

noticed by an actor called John Henderson, who gave a series of poetry readings at the Freemasons' Hall in London. Henderson's spirited rendering of the poem was rapturously received and Johnny Gilpin became the toast of London. By the last of Henderson's performances, John Wallis had boxes of John Gilpin puzzles on sale.

They were so successful that he searched for other stories to illustrate. In 1814 he came up with Defoe's *Robinson Crusoe*. Both subjects were copied and used by Wallis's competitors and successors for the rest of the century. John Betts published a composite Crusoe puzzle, made up from several illustrations; he included the usual book, but this time it contained an abridged version of the story, rather than a list of useful facts. Barfoot went one better in 1860 and produced a double-sided puzzle with John Gilpin on one side and Crusoe on the other. Gilpin's popularity declined after that, but *The Life and Strange Surprising Adventures of Robinson Crusoe* continued to fascinate manufacturers and their customers.

Nowadays, fairy tales would seem obvious subjects for children's publishing, but in the nineteenth century they were regarded with the deepest suspicion. Although unexpurgated fairy tales are full of cruelty, sex and violence, a few anonymous puzzle-makers, realizing their potential, used them for children's jigsaw puzzles. By 1860 the Barfoots had begun to produce charming puzzles showing some of the more acceptable scenes from fairy tales and, catalogued with didactic and religious puzzles, they soon became respectable.

The Bavarian toy-book package was especially suited to fairy tales, and Raphael Tuck published several in that format. But with the decline of toy-books and the invention of plywood fairy tales lost some of their appeal to jigsaw-makers. They were not to re-emerge until the advent of the cheap cardboard die-cut puzzles of the 1940s and '50s.

Jigsaws have always kept up with changing fashions in children's stories and the last fifty years have been dominated by Disney characters; Mickey Mouse, Donald Duck, Goofy and the rest have all been made into puzzles, and remain popular today. (Not all are intended for the very young, since some are large and very difficult to put together.) Moreover, since many children

William Tell. French alphabet puzzle c.1850.

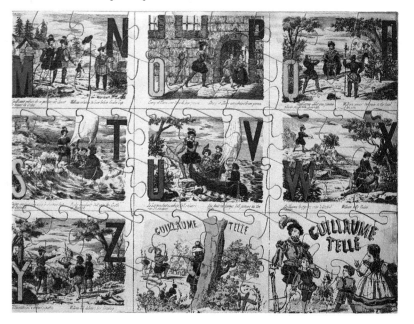

OLD MOTHER HUBBARD
Four of five puzzles from a puzzle box made in Bavaria.
Ernest Nister and E. P. Dutton *c.* 1895.

now prefer to watch television rather than to read a book, puzzle companies have used characters from programmes such as *The Magic Roundabout* and *The Muppets* to catch their interest. Some children, however, still enjoy puzzles based on classic stories: Raphael Tuck publish a series of wooden puzzles inspired by such old favourites as *Wind in the Willows, Alice Through the Looking Glass* and Alison Uttley's *Little Grey Rabbit*.

Nursery stories are not the only ones to have been used for jigsaws; with the rise of the murder story in the 1920s, some publishers packaged an uncompleted mystery novel with a jigsaw containing the solution. Harrap, for example, published a *Jigsaw Mystery Series*; each book consisted of 268 pages with a small 150-piece puzzle slotted into a folder at the back. In the same decade an American firm called Einson-Freeman made a series of 25-cent *Problem 'Jig Saw' Puzzles*. Clues to the mysteries were printed on the boxes, and the solutions could be found in the

Above: *Secret Tangles Mystery Book*. Many famous thriller writers contributed to this series of Mystery Puzzles published by Harrap.

Right: *Rip Van Winkle*. Raphael Tuck c. 1890. A toy-book package containing a double-sided chromolithographed puzzle and a story book.

completed puzzles. Detective stories and thrillers are now enjoying another wave of popularity, and the mystery jigsaw has had a revival. This time round, however, the puzzle is the major element and the clues are contained in a small booklet.

It seems that any successful book, television programme or moving picture is fair game for spin-off products, especially in the field of 'character merchandising'. Jigsaw manufacturers have benefited from this lucrative operation many times in the past and will no doubt continue to do so.

Rip and the queer men of the Mountains.

looking, he took a draught, and finding it good, another and another, till he became

RIP VAN WINKLE

FATHER TUCK'S NURSERY SERIES

ROBINSON CRUSOE
Sold and probably published by James Izzard. The style has a theatrical flavour
reminiscent of the toy theatre sets popular at that time. *c.* 1830.

NURSERY RHYMES FROM LITTLE BO-PEEP
This puzzle, from the toy book *Little Bo-Peep*, is double-sided. (The box label shows
Little Bo-Peep herself, though the puzzle does not.) Raphael Tuck *c*. 1890.

BROWNIE SCROLL PUZZLE
Skating by Palmer Cox, published by McLoughlin Brothers 1891.

MICKEY MOUSE
Jigsaw puzzle published by Chad Valley 'by arrangement with Walt Disney'.

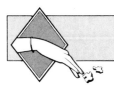

During the 1780s, before the storming of the Bastille, an anonymous English bookbinder demonstrated his sympathy for the victims of French oppression with a series of dissected puzzles. This was long before newspapers and magazines were illustrated, but from the pictures he bound into books he had come to understand the impact of a visual image;

Edward Oxford Firing at Her Majesty, in the Drive Leading From St. James's Park, June 10, 1840. A. Park c. 1841.

having bought up sets of small engravings, he dissected and packed them, two at a time, in small boxes to sell at 1s 6d each. One engraving showed the peaceful exterior of the Bastille, the other the grim, rat-infested filth of the dungeons. Nothing is known of the maker, but it is clear from the tiny, amateurish label on the box lid that he was a bookbinder; the labels read *The Bastile : Dissected Puzzle* and was printed, complete with spelling fault, using bookbinder's letters, not printer's type.

The French Revolution was obviously the talk of the day, and these were the first in a long tradition of current-events puzzles. Obviously topical puzzles had a short selling life, and so most of them were made by fly-by-night operators who used the cheapest possible engravings, cut in the most economical way. Royal occasions, from George IV's visit to Edinburgh in 1822 to Elizabeth II's Silver Jubilee in 1977, have always been popular subjects, but no one inspired more jigsaws than Queen Victoria.

As long as she was young and something of a novelty jigsaws recorded her public actions: in 1838 puzzles of her coronation flooded the market; later puzzles showed her receiving the Sword of State from the Lord Mayor; her marriage to Prince Albert; Edward Oxford's attempt to assassinate her while she was driving in St James's Park; accompanying Napoleon III to a banquet on his visit to London; even a domestic scene in the royal nursery. Jigsaws of royal engagements, weddings, coronations and anniversaries have appeared at regular intervals ever since. Silver Jubilee puzzles were among the most popular souvenirs in London during 1977.

Military victories were also recorded by puzzle-makers. In about 1845 an anonymous company published a jigsaw which became a spiral race game called *A New Game of Wellington's Victories*. All the Duke's victories were pictured, from Seringapatam in 1795 to the Battle of Waterloo in 1815, showing the Iron Duke himself, laurel-wreathed, at the top. Later there was the Storming of Sebastopol to celebrate, with a vigorous scene of young soldiers fighting their way to the town. And to prove that you cannot spoil a good story by retelling it, in the 1970s *The Times* published a jigsaw facsimile of its front page for 7 November 1805. It contained Collingwood's report of the victory at Trafalgar and the death of Nelson.

The Great Exhibition held in Hyde Park in 1851 was another very successful topic. Puzzles were put on sale long before the exhibition building, known as the Crystal Palace, was erected. Every puzzle claimed to be 'authentic' and quoted endless statistics about the revolutionary structure of the 'Palace'. During the year of the exhibition publishers approached the scene from various angles; several showed the grand opening by the Queen and Prince Albert, while others concentrated on the cosmopolitan crowds which thronged the exhibits. The most ingenious was an informative puzzle called *All the World and his Wife*, showing couples from cities all over the world; the height of the human figures was in direct proportion to the population of their cities, from London at $7\frac{1}{2}$ inches with a population of 2,800,000 down to Dresden at $\frac{1}{4}$ inch with a population of only 5,000.

The American equivalent of Britain's 1851 Exhibition was the World's Columbian Exposition, held at Jackson Park, Chicago in 1892. It was organized to celebrate the fourth centenary of Columbus's discovery of America. The jigsaw-makers had a

for children: included with their big, soft-covered toy-book were two very large, double-sided puzzles. The sinking of the Titanic may seem to have been a macabre subject for a plaything, but just as disaster movies have enormous success today, so disaster puzzles were once popular, and a puzzle depicting that scene was just one of them.

The Olympic Games too, have proved successful in jigsaw terms but for sheer volume of appropriate material, there has never been anything like the American space research programme. Puzzles have been made of the Apollo Moon Mission, the lift-off of rockets and eerie views of the Earth from outer space.

Top: *Indian Camp Scroll Puzzle*. McLoughlin Brothers 1894.

Above: *Chinese Gordon c.* 1885. A double-sided puzzle showing General Gordon on one side and a map of Egypt, Abyssinia and East Equatorial Africa on the other. Probably by Barfoot.

Right: *The Times 1805*. Published in the 1970s, cut from a facsimile of the front page reporting the death of Nelson at Trafalgar.

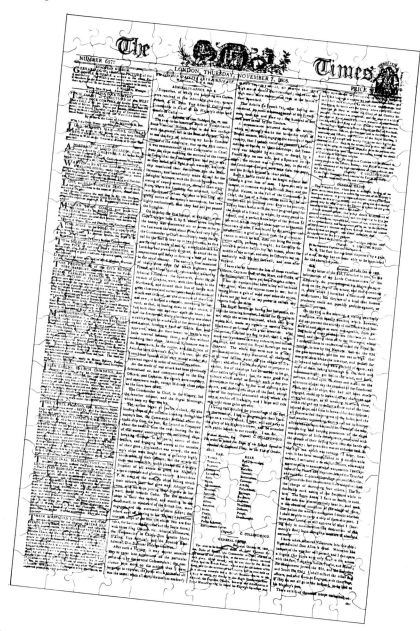

wealth of subjects to illustrate: the Machinery Hall, the Agricultural Hall, the Transportation Building, and so on. The famous Chicago store Marshall Field advertised three different puzzles of the exhibition that year.

Both disasters and outstanding human achievements have always been good themes for puzzle-makers. *Captain Ross' Voyage to the North Pole* inspired a vivid puzzle in 1833; later a fire in the small-arms store in the Tower of London in 1841 inspired an artist to paint a spirited picture of what might have happened, had the fire got out of hand, for an exciting jigsaw. Towards the end of the century the fantastic success of Stanley's book *In Darkest Africa* prompted Dean & Son to issue a version

THE PEOPLE'S ADVOCATE – LINCOLN
A Parker Brothers 'Pastime Puzzle' of more than 500 pieces.

THE HOUSE OF LORDS
Consisting of over 1,200 pieces and printed in twenty colours,
this puzzle cost 35 shillings. Raphael Tuck c. 1912.

VIEW OF THE AWFUL CONFLAGRATION AT THE TOWER OF LONDON
A view from Tower Hill of the Great Storehouse burning. It housed the
small-arms store which accidentally caught fire on 31 October 1841. An ideal
subject for the quick-witted jigsaw-maker. A. Park c. 1841.

THE LAST GRIP
A moving moment in a desert campaign makes a sensitive subject for this
unusually-cut puzzle. Manufacturer and artist unknown. Pre-1910.

CHARGE OF THE 21ST LANCERS AT OMDURMAN
From a set of photographically printed double-sided puzzles called
Soldiers of the Queen. Thomas Nelson *c*. 1900.

During this period we lost 69 men from starvation & sickness

Meeting of Stanley & Emin Pasha at Kavalti on Lake Albert Nyanza

Fight with Mazambonis people

STANLEY IN AFRICA
Two double-sided puzzles from a handsome set including a twelve-page book. Dean & Son c. 1890.

THE CORONATION OF QUEEN VICTORIA 1ST AT WESTMINSTER ABBEY, LONDON
(A. Park?) *c.* 1838.

SILVER JUBILEE
Chad Valley *c.* 1935.

T.R.H.'S PRINCESS ELIZABETH AND MARGARET ROSE
Based on a photograph by Marcus Adams. Chad Valley 1935.

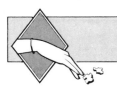

Hood's Rainy Day Puzzle c. 1809. Double-sided cardboard puzzle offered free to purchasers of Hood's Sarsaparilla.

I n the 1890s an American company called Hood decided to offer a free double-sided jigsaw puzzle to anyone who sent in three wrappers from their cure-all medicine, 'Sarsaparilla'. *Hood's Rainy Day Puzzle* was the first of a long line of advertising and propaganda jigsaws. It not only persuaded potential customers to choose Hood's sarsaparilla in preference to any other brand, but also carried the company's advertisement into their homes.

The Americans were way ahead of the British at that time, having mastered the cheap, die-cut technique of cardboard puzzle-manufacture. In 1905 the *Boston Sunday Globe* bore witness to another idea; given away with the newspaper was an uncut puzzle of two children bathing their dolls, with instructions to 'cut on black lines – mix pieces – then put them together'. But by the time of the great jigsaw craze in the 1920s the British had caught on. The manufacturers of John Knight's Soap reproduced and die-cut their famous poster of a grinning soot-blackened sweep saying 'You should see me on Sundays', while Pear's soap produced alternative puzzles: one a large, well-made and expensively produced picture, the other a crude, postcard-size reproduction of Millais's *Bubbles*. The importers of Mazawattee Tea also offered a cardboard die-cut version of one of their successful posters. Meanwhile in America the Continental Fire

Insurance Company of New York had decided to try jigsaw promotion. They commissioned a romanticized shipboard scene captioned 'First Stars and Stripes of the Ocean'.

Entertainers also made use of jigsaws to draw custom. Patrons of a London suburban cinema, showing Jackie Coogan in *Oliver Twist* in 1923, were given a cut-it-yourself cardboard puzzle of the famous child star. The Coliseum theatre followed in 1931 by offering small, well-made jigsaws of the whole cast of *White Horse Inn*. In 1936 an American company produced a series of 'Film-Star Puzzles'; made in the shape of a star, each of these featured a film-star (Moira Shearer, Robert Taylor and Laurel and Hardy were among those chosen) posed against a background of stills from popular films. Later Bertram Mills sponsored a series of cheap, but suitably gaudy, puzzles of his circus.

Jigsaws have also been used to raise the morale of troops at war, and to recruit combatants. The earliest recruiting puzzles were *The White Squadron* series published by McLoughlin Brothers in 1892; they made both jigsaws and block puzzles and

Amami c. 1920. Puzzle used to promote beauty aids in England.

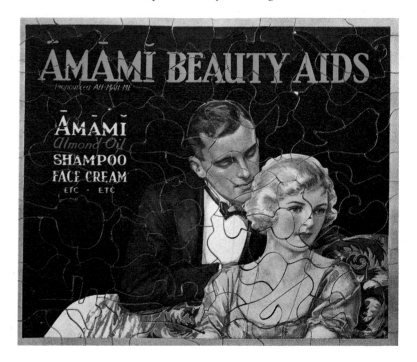

The Germans used several jigsaws during the First World War. There were pictures of the Kaiser and Hindenburg, and numerous battle scenes designed 'to while away the time during this exacting period'. During 1914 and 1915 they campaigned for American favour by means of battle scenes of the Eastern Front cut into jigsaws by P. Creutz, an American publisher. The same war provided the impetus for puzzles designed to inflame the French and spur them on to fight the Germans. There were jigsaws showing actual events such as the sinking of the *Lusitania and L'Allemagne a traitreusement attaqué la France Pacifique*. Another tactic was to show what might happen if the enemy triumphed; one horrifying series of puzzles was published showing German soldiers desecrating the peaceful French countryside and a German teacher flogging one of his pupils.

Some British internees at Gröningen produced their own war-time jigsaw. They were the 1,437 members of the First Naval Brigade who had escaped from the German advance on Antwerp in 1914. During their four years in Holland they made a lithographic view of the camp, mounted the prints and dissected them to sell in aid of camp funds. Another English puzzle, made in 1917 to help the Allied Cause, was unique in that it doubled as a hoop-la board.

The British Ministry of Information promoted several morale-raising jigsaws in 1940. They approved war artists' sketches of dramatic subjects such as *RAF Reconnaissance Planes beating off German Fighters, Ships in Convoy crossing the Atlantic*, and *The Navy driving off Nazi Bombers*, which were cut into popular puzzles.

Today, museums and art galleries play an important role in nurturing public interest in jigsaws. The first to do so was The London Museum during its 1968 exhibition 'Two Hundred Years of Jigsaw Puzzles'. Since then, museum jigsaw reproductions have become a common sight. London's Tate Gallery sells a series of postcard-sized jigsaws of famous paintings, and the British Museum offers a similar selection of puzzles showing popular exhibits. During the 1970s several commercial businesses have used jigsaw designs in their advertising graphics and there is little doubt that jigsaw puzzles and jigsaw imagery will continue to be used by organizations in search of persuaders.

Top: *Groningen POW Camp c.*1916. Made by some of the members of the First Naval Brigade interned during the First World War.

Above: *Winston Churchill, Man of Action c.*1944. From a set including a puzzle of Churchill as a 'Man of Vision'.

Right: *Jackie Coogan* 1923. A give-away puzzle promoting Jackie Coogan in *Oliver Twist*.

sold them with descriptive booklets. A set of six named vessels from the New Fleet of United States Men-of-War was 'selected to show best the new types of vessels being built for Uncle Sam which cannot fail to post boys on Naval Matters, as well as amuse them'. Puzzle-persuaders were used right up to the Second World War, when a jigsaw showing a group of pretty WRNS chatting to Admiral Mountbatten was made to attract girls into the service.

SUNNY JIM
One of a series of Sunny Jim trademark puzzles, advertising
Force breakfast cereal, made during the 1930s.

ILS ONT TORPILLÉ LE LUSITANIA ASSASSINANT D'INNOCENTES VICTIMES

FIRST WORLD WAR PROPAGANDA PUZZLES
Above: French puzzle captioned 'They have torpedoed the Lusitania'.
Right: *Hoopla in the Trenches*. This double-sided puzzle shows British troops playing hoopla in
the trenches, and its pieces are used to construct an actual hoopla game.
Except for the Kaiser and Tirpitz, most of the figures in the picture are symbolic.
Far right: *Kaiser Wilhelm II*. German puzzle with a characteristic cutting
pattern, captioned 'Whiling away the time during hard times'.

A WEDDING IN CATLAND
One of Hood's Sarsaparilla promotion puzzles, using an
illustration by Louis Wain. *c.* 1900.

UNCLE SAM IN THE PACIFIC 1908
Advertising toothpaste at a time of much American activity in the Pacific.

PEARS SOAP
A good-quality wooden puzzle for discreet advertising.

JIG-O-LOTTO
A jigsaw 'Lotto' game for four players, advertising John Knight's soap products. The box includes four puzzles with numbered pieces and numbered pattern sheets.

SUNNY JIM
Showing Sir Malcolm Campbell's record-breaking Rolls-Royce
Campbell Blue Bird Car in 1933.

R.M.S. QUEEN MARY

The climax of express passenger ships of huge dimensions was reached in the making of
this ship and her sister craft the *Queen Elizabeth*. Queen Mary launched the ship bearing
her name in 1934, and the liner entered service in 1936. Weighing 81,237 tons gross,
she is 1,019 feet long. Her average speed was 28.5 knots, and she could accommodate
2,038 passengers (first-class, cabin and tourist); in World War II she served as a
troopship carrying up to 10,500 men per voyage. Now she is moored permanently at
Long Beach, California as a tourist attraction.

Puzzle made by Chad Valley for the Cunard White Star Line.

TOM KITTEN

Beatrix Potter's *Tale of Tom Kitten*, number 8 in a series of twenty-three, was published
in September 1907. At this stage in her career, Beatrix Potter inclined more to
watercolour than to line illustration, and this painting is a charming example of her
style. In the book Tom Kitten is the son of Tabitha Twitchit, brother to Mittens and
Moppet, and the story tells of how he managed to ruin the smart blue outfit he is
wearing in the picture.

Beatrix Potter (28 July 1866 to 22 December 1943) lived and worked in the Lake District.

Puzzle published in 1934 by Frederick Warne & Co. Ltd.

INDEX

ACKNOWLEDGEMENTS

The author and publisher are grateful to the following for permission to
reproduce puzzles and illustrative material:
Blaise Castle House Museum, Henbury, Bristol, page 89;
Institut Pédagogique National, Collections Historiques, Paris,
pages 37, 64 right and 84;
Museum of London, pages 38 right, 53, 55 below, 57, 59 below, 63,
73 right, 77 and 83 below left;
Norfolk Museums Service, Strangers Hall Museum, Norwich, pages 19 above,
28 right, 38 left, 43, 52, 56 above left, 73 below left and 79;
RKO General Pictures, pages 6–7;
Herbert J. Siegel, pages 70, 73 above left, 86 and 87;
John Solloway, pages 56 below left and 91;
The Margaret Woodbury Strong Museum, page 54 right.

Queen Mary jigsaw puzzle, reproduced by kind permission of The Palitoy Company.
Tom Kitten jigsaw puzzle, illustration by Beatrix Potter, reproduced
by kind permission of Frederick Warne and Co. Ltd.

All other puzzles are from the author's personal collection.

Cover illustration by Mick Brownfield.

THE AUTHOR

London-born Linda Hannas, who is married to a Norwegian, lived for a time in Norway before returning to England with her husband. A little over twenty years ago they set up an antiquarian book business in Bromley, Kent. Her interest in old jigsaw puzzles began when she found early examples in secondhand bookshops, stacked alongside early children's books. When she discovered a puzzle dating back to the eighteenth century, her interest intensified, and she began trying to find out more about them. Her first task was to track down the inventor of the jigsaw puzzle, John Spilsbury, and from there her researches, and her collection of old puzzles, grew apace.

The Hannas Collection, which includes all kinds of printed toys as well as jigsaws, now boasts about 500 puzzles. The London Museum's exhibition 'Two Hundred Years of Jigsaw Puzzles', held in 1968, was largely based on these, and the catalogue was written by Linda Hannas.

She has taken part in various radio and television programmes, among them one featuring the collection (*Dissected Maps and Pictures* in the BBC Television series *Victorian Pastimes*).

Her reference book *The English Jigsaw Puzzle 1790 to 1890* (Wayland) appeared in 1972.